# Revenge

# Revenge

*Essential Literary Themes*

by Caitlin Ray

Essential Library

An Imprint of Abdo Publishing | abdopublishing.com

abdopublishing.com

Published by Abdo Publishing, a division of ABDO, PO Box 398166, Minneapolis, Minnesota 55439. Copyright © 2016 by Abdo Consulting Group, Inc. International copyrights reserved in all countries. No part of this book may be reproduced in any form without written permission from the publisher. Essential Library™ is a trademark and logo of Abdo Publishing.

Printed in the United States of America, North Mankato, Minnesota
042015
092015

Cover Photo: Shutterstock Images
Interior Photos: Shutterstock Images, 1; Everett Collection, 13, 20, 67, 69, 77; Bettmann/ Corbis, 15, 43; Wilfrid Newton/Universal Pictures/Photofest, 16, 18, 33; World History Archive/Newscom, 22; AP Images, 25; Two Cities/Rank/Newscom, 27; Claudio Divizia/ Shutterstock Images, 31; Columbia/Everett Collection, 35; Everett Historical/Shutterstock Images, 41; iStockphoto, 45, 49, 51; Harry Clarke, 47; Sunset Boulevard/Corbis, 59; Lorey Sebastian/Paramount Pictures/Everett Collection, 61, 63, 73; Paramount Pictures/ Newscom, 71; Paramount Home Entertainment/Newscom, 75; 20th Century Fox Film Corp./Everett Collection, 83, 85, 86, 89, 92, 95

Editor: Jenna Gleisner
Series Designer: Maggie Villaume

**Library of Congress Control Number: 2015931036**
**Cataloging-in-Publication Data**

Ray, Caitlin.
 Revenge / Caitlin Ray.
  p. cm. -- (Essential literary themes)
Includes bibliographical references and index.
ISBN 978-1-62403-808-2
1. American literature--Themes, motives--Juvenile literature.  2. American literature--History and criticism--Juvenile literature.   I. Title.
810--dc23

                                      2015931036

# Contents

## 1

INTRODUCTION TO

# Themes in Literature

*D*o you find yourself drawn to the same types of stories? Are your favorite characters on a quest? Are they seeking revenge? Or are your favorite stories about love? Love, revenge, a quest—these are all examples of themes. Although each story is different, many stories focus on similar themes. You can expand your understanding of the books you read by recognizing the common themes within them.

## What Is a Theme?

A theme is a concept or idea that shows up again and again in various works of art, literature, music, theater, film, and other endeavors throughout history. Some themes revolve around a story's plot. For example, a play about a young girl moving away from home and learning the ways of the world would be considered a coming of age story. But themes are not always so easily noticed. For example, a work might have allusions. Allusions are references, sometimes indirect, to other works or historical events. Themes might also relate to specific characters or subjects of a work. For example, many stories present heroes or villains. These common character types are often called archetypes.

## How Do You Uncover a Theme?

Themes are presented in different ways in different works, so you may not always be aware of them. Many works have multiple themes. Uncover themes by asking yourself questions about the work. What is the main point or lesson of the story? What is the main conflict? What do the characters want? Where does the story take place? In many cases, themes may not be apparent until after a close study, or analysis, of the text.

## What Is an Analysis?

Writing an analysis allows you to explore the themes in a work. In an analysis, you can consider themes in multiple ways. You can describe what themes are present in a work. You can compare one work to another to see how the presentation of a theme differs between the two forms. You can see how the use of a particular theme either supports or rejects society's norms. Rather than attempt to discover the author's purpose in creating a work, an analysis reveals what *you* see in the work.

Raising your awareness of themes through analysis allows you to dive deeper into the work itself. You may begin to see similarities between all creative works that you encounter. You may also improve your own writing by expanding your understanding of how stories use themes to engage readers.

## Forming a Thesis

Form your questions about how a theme is presented in a work or multiple works and find answers within the work itself. Then you can create a thesis. The thesis is the key point in your analysis. It is your argument about the work. For example, if you want to argue that the theme of a book is love, your thesis could be worded as follows: Allison Becket's novel *On the Heartless Road* asserts that receiving love is critical to the human experience.

### How to Make a Thesis Statement

In an analysis, a thesis statement typically appears at the end of the introductory paragraph. It is usually only one sentence long and states the author's main idea.

## Providing Evidence

Once you have formed a thesis, you must provide evidence to support it. Evidence will usually take the form of examples and quotations from the work itself, often including dialogue from a character. You may wish to address what others have written about the work. Quotes from these individuals may help support your claim. If you find any quotes or examples that contradict your thesis, you will need to create an argument against them. For instance: Many critics claim the theme of love is secondary to that of revenge, as the main character, Carly, sabotages the lives of her loved ones throughout the novel. However, the novel's resolution proves that Carly's experience with love is the key to her humanity.

## Concluding the Essay

After you have written several arguments and included evidence to support them, finish the essay with

## How to Support a Thesis Statement

An analysis should include several arguments that support the thesis's claim. An argument is one or two sentences long and is supported by evidence from the work being discussed. Organize the arguments into paragraphs. These paragraphs make up the body of the analysis.

a conclusion. The conclusion restates the ideas from the thesis and summarizes some of the main points from the essay. The conclusion's final thought often considers additional implications for the essay or gives the reader something to ponder further.

## In This Book

In this book, you will read summaries of works, each followed by an analysis. Critical thinking sections will give you a chance to consider other theses and questions about the work. Did you agree with the author's analysis? What other questions are raised by the thesis and its arguments? You can also see other directions the author could have pursued to analyze the work. Then, in the Analyze It section in the final pages of this book, you will have an opportunity to create your own analysis paper.

# The Theme of Revenge

The book you are reading focuses on the theme of revenge. Revenge is a common theme in works of literature and drama, as everyone experiences unfairness in life. However, while the desire for revenge is universal, works of art explore how taking revenge, especially when it is violent, can cause chaos. Francis Bacon, an English essayist of the 1500s, wrote "revenge is a kind of wild justice," and the more we desire revenge, the more laws we need to control our desire.[1] The theme of revenge explores what happens when we let our desire for vengeance override those laws.

## Look for the Guides

Throughout the chapters that analyze the works, thesis statements have been highlighted. The box next to the thesis helps explain what questions are being raised about the work. Supporting arguments have also been highlighted. The boxes next to the arguments help explain how these points support the thesis. The conclusions are also accompanied by explanatory boxes. Look for these guides throughout each analysis.

## 2

AN OVERVIEW OF

# *Hamlet* and *Othello*

R evenge was a common theme in works of literature and theater during the Renaissance period in England. *Hamlet* is perhaps William Shakespeare's best-known play and is an example of a revenge tragedy. *Hamlet* has a far-reaching legacy, enjoying a long production history since its first performance in the early 1600s. *Hamlet*, and its theme of revenge, continues to speak to our generation and generations to come.

## *Hamlet* Summary in Brief

The tragedy *Hamlet* begins with Horatio, Hamlet's close friend, and other soldiers seeing the ghost of the king who just died. Horatio decides to tell Hamlet, prince of

Hamlet seeks revenge for the murder of his father.

Denmark and son to the late king, about the sighting. As midnight approaches, Hamlet also sees the ghost. The ghost assures Hamlet he is indeed his father and that Hamlet's uncle, Claudius, murdered him by pouring poison into his ear while he slept. Claudius is now king and has also married Hamlet's mother. Hamlet's father urges Hamlet to avenge his death.

Hamlet begins taking on an odd, even mad, behavior. Polonius, the king's adviser, declares the cause of Hamlet's behavior is his love for Ophelia, Polonius's daughter. A group of theater actors arrive at the castle to perform the next night, and Hamlet convinces them to put on a play about a murder. Once alone, Hamlet talks to himself and reveals his plan: he has been acting mad while gathering evidence of his uncle's guilt. He decides to give the actors a specific scene to act out, one in which a king is poisoned by his brother while sleeping. Hamlet hopes to "catch the conscience of the king" and see King Claudius looking guilty as he watches the scene play out.[1]

## Gathering Proof

While the actors begin performing the scene of the king's murder, Hamlet closely watches the king and

During the play, Hamlet, *left*, watches the king's reaction for signs of guilt.

queen. King Claudius becomes upset and abruptly leaves. Hamlet then finds King Claudius praying alone. In his prayers, King Claudius confesses to murdering his brother. Even though Hamlet has proof of Claudius's guilt, he decides not to murder Claudius at that moment. If he were to kill the king in the middle of prayer and confession, Claudius might ascend to heaven. Hamlet, in a soliloquy, reasons he would rather kill Claudius in the midst of sin so Claudius might be punished in the afterlife. Hamlet then finds his mother and advances on her, saying she should not have married Claudius. At this moment, Polonius, who was meeting with the

Hamlet decides to spare King Claudius's life while Claudius prays.

queen prior to Hamlet's arrival, calls out from his hiding place behind the curtains. Hamlet mistakes Polonius for Claudius, stabbing the curtains and killing Polonius.

Queen Gertrude finds King Claudius and reports to him that Hamlet has killed Polonius. King Claudius then sends Hamlet to England as punishment. Meanwhile, out in the fields of Denmark, Fortinbras, the prince of Norway, sends a message to the court that he plans to invade Denmark. Queen Gertrude and King Claudius observe Ophelia's mad behavior caused by the death of her father, Polonius. A messenger enters, announcing Laertes, Polonius's son who has been away, has returned to the castle. Laertes insists on confronting Hamlet for the murder of his father. The queen then announces Ophelia has just drowned herself.

## Revenge in Death

Hamlet returns from England to find Ophelia has died. He reveals himself to Laertes, and after their fight is broken up, they promise to meet again for a duel. Laertes and King Claudius, preparing for Hamlet's arrival, spike their swords and goblets of wine with poison. Hamlet and Laertes then fight before the court. Queen Gertrude drinks from a poisoned goblet,

Queen Gertrude, who drinks from a poisoned goblet, is also killed as a result of revenge.

originally meant for Hamlet, and dies. Laertes, first wounding Hamlet, is then cut by his own sword's poisoned blade and dies. Hamlet, in his last breath, stabs Claudius with the poisoned sword, getting his revenge right before he himself dies. As he dies, Hamlet begs Horatio to tell his story. Fortinbras enters the scene, having successfully invaded Denmark. Horatio explains what has happened, and Fortinbras decrees Hamlet will be buried as a soldier and hero.

## *Othello* Synopsis

Shakespeare's *Othello*, written around 1604, is another play with a major theme of revenge. Similar to *Hamlet*, *Othello*'s influence has reached far beyond the Elizabethan stage. *Othello* has a different interpretation of revenge. Rather than following the main character as the avenger, as in *Hamlet*, *Othello*'s audience sees the antagonist plotting revenge.

*Othello* begins with Iago, a soldier, discussing the promotion of a third soldier, Cassio, over him. Othello, a general, made the decision. In retaliation, Iago makes public the news that Othello has eloped with Desdemona, a prominent daughter of a senator. Desdemona's father finds out but, upon hearing the

Iago's plan backfires as Desdemona's father, *center*, acknowledges Desdemona's love and marriage to Othello, *left*.

elopement was consensual, decides to embrace the marriage. He takes Othello to the Duke of Venice in order to have him rule on the legality of the elopement. Othello must then go with the troops to Cyprus to protect it from the Turkish army, leaving Desdemona behind. Iago, still angry about not receiving a promotion, decides to convince Othello that Desdemona is cheating on him with Cassio in order to see revenge on both men.

## Plotting Revenge

Later, in Cyprus, a storm has caused the Turkish fleet to retreat in their advance. Othello is also caught in the storm. While waiting for him to return, Desdemona flirts with Cassio. Iago begins his scheme, planting the idea of Cassio and Desdemona having an affair to the other soldiers. When Othello finally arrives, he holds a celebration for both the Turkish retreat and his marriage to Desdemona. Under the guise of celebration, Iago provokes Cassio into drinking too much wine. Inebriated, Cassio starts a fight with the other soldiers. Othello then demotes Cassio as punishment for fighting. Iago secretly reassures Cassio he can restore his reputation. He suggests Cassio ask Desdemona to convince Othello he should get his job back. Iago brings his wife Emilia, Desdemona's attendant, into the scheme, asking her to convince Desdemona to argue on Cassio's behalf.

Desdemona meets with Cassio and decides to talk to Othello for him. Desdemona hears Othello coming, and Cassio, nervous about Desdemona's conversation about him, quickly leaves. Iago, who is with Othello, remarks on how suspicious Cassio's sudden departure

Iago uses alcohol to outwit Cassio to get his revenge.

from Desdemona looks. Othello, meanwhile, agrees to reinstate Cassio to please Desdemona. Iago then asks Othello to notice Desdemona's behavior with Cassio. He notes how Desdemona deceived her father in marrying Othello, so it is possible she may try to deceive others as well. Emilia then steals Desdemona's handkerchief and gives it to Iago, who ensures Cassio has it. Iago lies to Othello, claiming he has seen Cassio with Desdemona's handkerchief. This news enrages Othello, and he suffers from an epileptic fit. He finds Desdemona, and asks for the handkerchief. She, having dropped it earlier, does not have it. Later, Cassio gives Bianca, Cassio's mistress, Desdemona's handkerchief.

Othello and Iago discuss the meaning of Desdemona's lost handkerchief. Iago tells Othello to hide and watch Cassio's reactions while he talks with Cassio about Desdemona. Othello hides, while Iago proceeds to ask Cassio about Bianca in a way that makes it sound as if he is talking about Desdemona. During their discussion, Bianca suddenly appears and gives the handkerchief back to Cassio, insulted because it is clearly another woman's. Othello realizes the handkerchief is Desdemona's and is convinced of the affair. He then plots to murder Desdemona, and Iago suggests he strangle her in their bed while Iago murders Cassio.

## Revenge Gone Wrong

Cassio again fights other soldiers and becomes gravely injured. Meanwhile, Othello enters his bedroom where Desdemona has fallen asleep while waiting for him. He then smothers her with a pillow. Emilia runs in too late and tells Othello that Iago lied to him about Desdemona's affair with Cassio. Upon the discovery of Desdemona's body, Emilia calls out, gathering everyone to see what Othello has done. As Othello attempts to justify his actions by relating news of the affair between Desdemona and Cassio, Emilia realizes it is the handkerchief she found that Iago used as proof of the affair. Iago then stabs and kills his wife and runs out of the room with others in pursuit. They tie up Iago and bring him back, along with the injured Cassio. Iago's deceit is then unraveled, and Othello stabs himself and dies. Those in attendance agree that Iago must be punished for his evil deeds.

Ultimately, Iago's plan of revenge ends in Othello's murder of Desdemona.

## 3

# Vengeful Characters

The revenge tragedy genre refers specifically to a type of tragedy popularized and performed in Elizabethan England from approximately 1587 to 1642. Plays of this genre often depict a main character who becomes obsessed with revenge, and ultimately, that desire for revenge leads to the main character's downfall. Revenge tragedies deal specifically with blood feuds, which often begin and end with violent acts, such as murder, against either the individual or the family. The people of Elizabethan England were very interested in themes of revenge, especially because this was a time of transition from older, feudal laws to a court-based judicial system. Murder became illegal no matter the circumstance and no matter if the family had a blood

Violent acts were a common theme of revenge tragedies in Elizabethan England.

feud or not. Revenge tragedies reflected this change, and characters seeking revenge often died as a result.

## Blood Feuds to Rules of Law

*Hamlet* and *Othello,* both revenge tragedies, take into account the role of revenge in Elizabethan life. The literary criticism of new historicism considers a work of literature within the context of the historical period in which it was created. New historicist analyses can also consider other events that might have shaped the cultural attitudes of the author or the audience. Hamlet and Iago are two characters who seek revenge very differently. Both acts of revenge reflect changing attitudes in Elizabethan England.

During the Elizabethan era, there was a transition from a belief in blood feuds, in which revenge was sought because someone wronged someone else, to justice being found in a court of law, where evidence was needed to prove a person's innocence or guilt. Iago, representing the earlier type of blood feuds, is seen as a morally wrong character, whereas Hamlet, who seeks evidence before acting on revenge, is portrayed as sympathetic. Because Hamlet seeks proof and is reluctant to find revenge, he is ultimately regarded as a hero, whereas Iago, whose motives are purely selfish, is portrayed as a revengeful traitor.

Iago and Hamlet have very different motives for seeking revenge against those who have wronged them. Hamlet's motive is avenging the murder of his father, whereas Iago's motive is anger and jealousy. Since Hamlet's motive for revenge is based on getting payback for his family's name and honor, Hamlet is portrayed as sympathetic. Also, Hamlet behaves more rationally, seeking proof the king murdered his father before acting on his revenge. Therefore, the audience, believing in the law and order of the courts, can sympathize with Hamlet as he struggles to find proof throughout the play.

## Thesis

The thesis for this essay states: "Because Hamlet seeks proof and is reluctant to find revenge, he is ultimately regarded as a hero, whereas Iago, whose motives are purely selfish, is portrayed as a revengeful traitor."
This essay will illustrate the reasons why audiences of the time would have viewed Hamlet as a hero and Iago as a traitor.

## Argument One

The author makes the first argument of the essay: "Iago and Hamlet have very different motives for seeking revenge against those who have wronged them." The author then argues why the two characters' forms of revenge are different.

Hamlet's impulse is pure. He hopes to give his father eternal rest.

In contrast, Iago's impulse is purely internal, as he is motivated by his own jealousy after another man receives a promotion he feels he deserves. Iago speaks of this internal desire for revenge when devising his plan: "The thought whereof/Doth, like a poisonous mineral, gnaw my inwards; And nothing can or shall content my soul / Till I am even'd with him."[1] An internal desire for revenge indicates selfishness in Iago's character.

## Argument Two

The second argument states: "The difference between Hamlet and Iago is reinforced through their ability to act—or not to act—in favor of their desires." The author compares the actions of both Hamlet and Iago in this argument.

The difference between Hamlet and Iago is reinforced through their ability to act—or not to act—in favor of their desires. Hamlet constantly second-guesses himself, leading to inaction throughout the play. This is in contrast to Iago, who constantly acts toward his plan of revenge. Hamlet's various monologues to the audience reveal his hesitance to act. In Hamlet's famous "to be, or not to be" speech, he thinks aloud: "Conscience

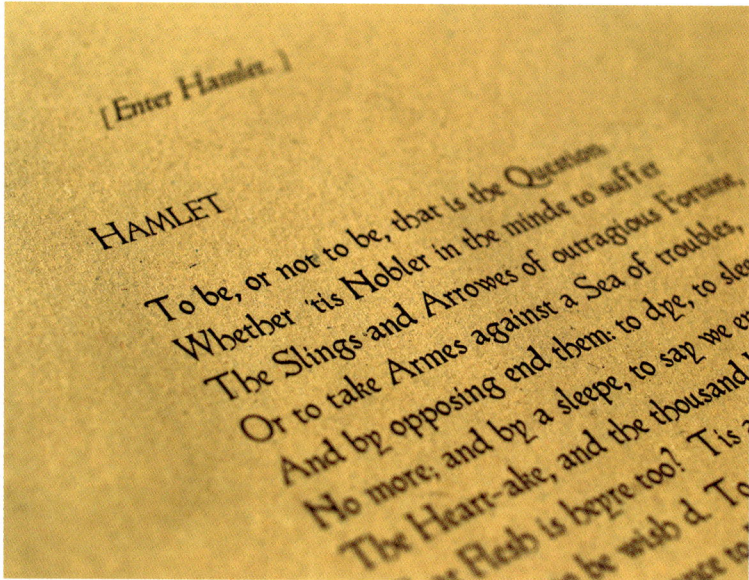

[Enter Hamlet.]

HAMLET

To be, or not to be, that is the Question:
Whether 'tis Nobler in the minde to suffer
The Slings and Arrowes of outragious Fortune,
Or to take Armes against a Sea of troubles,
And by opposing end them: to dye, to slee
No more; and by a sleepe, to say we en
The Heart-ake, and the thousand
Flesh is heyre too! Tis a
be wish'd. To
ge to

Hamlet's famous speech illustrates his inner turmoil.

does make cowards of us all / And thus the native hue of resolution / Is sicklied o'er with the pale cast of thought."[2] Here, Hamlet is aware his conscience makes him incapable of acting. Because Hamlet is considering suicide, a morally wrong action, his hesitance makes him sympathetic to the audience, who is listening in on his internal thoughts. The audience can hear as Hamlet struggles with the circumstances around him.

While Iago also delivers monologues to the audience, his monologues do not reveal an internal struggle. Instead, they show Iago's desire for vengeance, making him a less sympathetic character. For example, in the first scene of *Othello*, Iago discusses his anger toward

Othello and his plan to act loyal to him while also planning his revenge: "Though I do hate [Othello] as I do hell-pains / Yet, for necessity of present life / I must show out a flag and sign of love / Which is indeed but sign."[3] The audience immediately sees hate motivates Iago. He will work through deception to get revenge on Othello, no matter what evidence may be offered that Othello made the right decision in promoting Cassio. The audience sees Iago will not waver in his thinking.

## Argument Three

The third argument evaluates the ways in which readers are left to think about Hamlet and Othello at the end of their respective plays. The argument states: "While both *Hamlet* and *Othello* end in acts of revenge, the final scenes in both plays further reveal the differences between the characters of Hamlet and Iago."

While both *Hamlet* and *Othello* end in acts of revenge, the final scenes in both plays further reveal the differences between the characters of Hamlet and Iago. *Hamlet*'s final scene includes a sword battle between Hamlet and Laertes. In this scene, Laertes and all of the members of Hamlet's family—including Hamlet, King Claudius, and Queen Gertrude—die after either drinking poison or being stabbed by a poisoned sword.

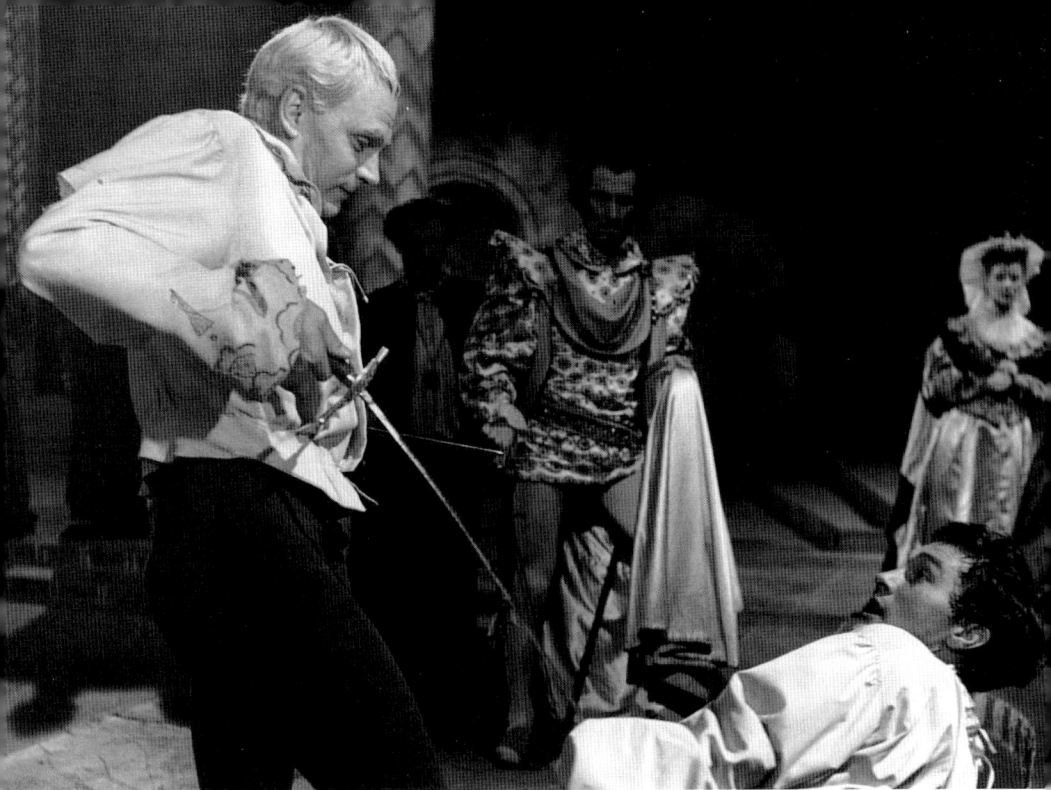

Although Hamlet's revenge results in murder and his own death, he is pronounced a hero at the end of the play.

Hamlet gets his vengeance against his uncle, but, in doing so, he destroys his entire family. His death, however, is treated with respect, as Prince Fortinbras, who takes over the kingdom, decrees Hamlet should be treated as a soldier who died in battle because he "proved [himself] most royal."[4] Respect is given to Hamlet by those still alive at the end of the play because Hamlet's decision, while not perfect, was made rationally according to standards of law at the time.

However, Iago is not afforded the same kind of respect for his actions at the end of *Othello*. After the other soldiers discover Iago's plot, Othello kills himself in grief, and Iago is blamed for both Desdemona and Othello's tragic ends. Iago is regarded as a "hellish villain" and is to be punished for their deaths.[5] Iago's ultimate fate is punishment by the legal representative (the lord governor). He is treated as nothing more than a "dog" for his actions.[6]

## Argument Four

The author's final argument states: "Both *Hamlet* and *Othello* were written and performed for Elizabethan audiences in the early 1600s, reflecting the differing opinions Elizabethan citizens would have held had these events happened to them." This argument further justifies the audience's sympathies.

Both *Hamlet* and *Othello* were written and performed for Elizabethan audiences in the early 1600s, reflecting the differing opinions Elizabethan citizens would have held had these events happened to them. According to *Hamlet* scholar Eleanor Prosser, the official view of Elizabethan law was that private revenge was forbidden, and courts should resolve disputes between people.[7] However, the popular opinion of the Elizabethan people was that if a wrong was done to someone, particularly murder, that person's family was justified in seeking revenge. Hamlet's reluctance and desire for proof would have resonated with an

Iago, whose motives were based on jealousy and greed, would not have had audiences' sympathy.

## Conclusion

In the conclusion, the author reminds readers of the thesis: while both Hamlet and Iago are seeking their revenge, they go about doing so in different ways. The author then summarizes the main points in the essay and attempts to connect them to the audience. The author claims these plays allow the audience to consider their own opinions on revenge.

Elizabethan audience, who would have felt the conflict between the English state and popular opinion. Between Hamlet and Iago, audience sympathies would have sided much more with Hamlet, who sought evidence and was called to action by his father's ghost.

Both *Othello* and *Hamlet* exemplify the theme of revenge, yet they do so in different ways. Hamlet, seeking to avenge his father's murder, spends much of the first two acts of the play considering the morality of what he might do and gathering proof of King Claudius's guilt. Iago, on the other hand, spends most of his time acting on vengeful plots against Othello. In the end, however, both Hamlet and Iago are the cause of several deaths and receive consequences for those deaths. While each character goes about revenge in different ways, the common theme allows audience members to reflect on their own ideas of revenge and its dangers.

# Thinking Critically

Now it's your turn to assess the essay. Consider these questions:

1. Do you agree with the author's central claim that Hamlet is regarded as a hero and Iago as a traitor? Why, or why not?

2. How does Hamlet's killing of Polonius fit into this argument? Does it provide a counterargument to the main claim?

3. Who still lives by the end of these plays? Why do you think they live while many of the main characters do not?

# Other Approaches

Scholars have written about *Hamlet* and *Othello* in a number of ways. Some of the other ways to analyze *Hamlet* and *Othello* are through the roles of women in each character's revenge plot, as well as how the body is portrayed.

## Feminist Analysis

In *Hamlet* and *Othello*, the two prominent female characters, Ophelia and Desdemona, both die. Ophelia, who dies by drowning, is driven mad because of her father's death. Desdemona is killed because of Othello's suspicion that she is cheating. A possible thesis that considers the role of women within the plays' theme of revenge might be: Both Desdemona and Ophelia become innocent victims of the male characters' quests for revenge, supporting the attitude of the time that women are passive and do not fight back in the face of violence.

## Disability Analysis

Disability criticism considers the role of bodies, mentally and physically, within literature and film. In *Hamlet* and *Othello*, disability plays an important role—both when Ophelia becomes mad and kills herself and when Othello falls into an epileptic fit. A thesis that might reflect the importance of the body in these plays might be: In *Othello* and *Hamlet*, characters' bodies often physically change as a result of their emotional states, and this physical response highlights the effects of revenge on these characters.

## 4

AN OVERVIEW OF

# "The Cask of Amontillado"

$\mathcal{E}$dgar Allen Poe was born in 1809 to traveling actors. Both of his parents died early in his childhood, after which Poe was sent to Richmond, Virginia, to live with a rich benefactor, John Allan. Despite Allan's attempts to make Poe into a proper southern gentleman and businessman, Poe was not interested in such work. Instead, he aspired to be a writer.

After a few failed attempts at attending college, Poe moved to New York City and began a career working as a writer and editor of literary journals. He worked in this profession until the end of his short life in 1849. He lived at first with his aunt, Maria Poe Clemm, and cousin, Virginia. Poe fell in love with Virginia, and the

Many of Poe's poems and short stories focus on the theme of revenge.

couple married. At this time, he also began working as an editor and critic, while publishing his own works as well. He worked at a variety of literary journals throughout his life, at times making good money, yet he was completely poor at other times. Near the end of his life, Poe started becoming famous for his poems. Poe's short stories and poems include themes of revenge and the macabre. His works have become part of popular culture, particularly the poem "The Raven" and the short story "The Tell-Tale Heart." His short story "The Cask of Amontillado" strongly features revenge.

## Romanticism

Poe is considered a part of the romantic literary tradition of the early to mid-1800s. Romanticism started in Europe and spread through North America from approximately 1830 to the American Civil War era (1861–1865). Romantics believed in freedom from authority and felt the individual's perspective on life was more important than a collective group's perspective. They often believed feelings were visible in outer experiences and settings, a theme seen in "The Tell-Tale Heart," "The Cask of Amontillado," and other works by Poe. For example, the guilt of the main character

Poe is perhaps best known for his poem "The Raven."

in "The Tell-Tale Heart" is represented by the constant heartbeat the main character hears in the floor.

## A Summary of "The Cask of Amontillado"

"The Cask of Amontillado," a short story published in 1846, has been continuously in print since its publication. In "The Cask of Amontillado," the narrator and main character, Montresor, seeks revenge against a man named Fortunato for reasons never explained in the story. Montresor believes he must punish Fortunato and devises a plan to do so. He decides to exploit Fortunato's weakness—his love and knowledge of wine—in order to take advantage of Fortunato. Both men attend a carnival-themed party, where Montresor spots Fortunato, who is wearing a jester costume with bells. Montresor lures Fortunato away from the party with a promise to show him a cask of amontillado, a type of Spanish sherry, or wine. The men go into Montresor's catacombs, where the cask is kept. As they continue past the bones of Montresor's ancestors, Montresor repeatedly suggests they turn back and forget the wine. He claims he can get someone else's opinion of the wine. In doing so, Montresor allows Fortunato opportunities to escape and manipulates Fortunato into going farther into the catacombs.

## Fortunato's Downfall

Fortunato accepts more wine from Montresor and grows increasingly drunk. While Fortunato's judgment is impaired, Montresor chains the man inside a crypt. The intoxicated Fortunato does not react, and Montresor quickly begins closing the crypt by walling it up with plaster and brick. As he does so, Fortunato begins to laugh, commenting on the good joke he thinks

Montresor leads Fortunato down into his catacombs, where skeletons of his deceased family members populate the walls.

Montresor is playing on him. Finally, Montresor tosses a torch into the crypt. He listens for sounds from Fortunato but only hears jingling bells from the man's jester costume. He comments, "My heart grew sick; it was the dampness of the catacombs that made it so."[1] Montresor, ignoring what could be a feeling of guilt, ends the story by stating, "For the half of a century no mortal has disturbed them. In pace requiescat [may he rest in peace]!"[2] He successfully got his revenge, and his crime was never discovered.

# 5

# Symbolic Revenge

In Poe's "The Cask of Amontillado," the character Montresor seeks revenge against Fortunato, although the reasons for his doing so are never revealed. Throughout the text, however, there are a variety of symbols that foreshadow Montresor's revenge. Through these symbols, readers can predict Fortunato's grisly end. Symbolism can often help readers make sense of the text, and literature often depends on symbols, metaphors, and images to communicate with the audience. Symbols stand for something else. There is often a universal meaning to symbols in literature. For example, the symbol of flowing water often suggests the passing of time. Finding symbols can bring deeper meaning and understanding of the events of a text.

From Fortunato's outfit to his place of death, "The Cask of Amontillado" is full of revengeful symbolism.

## Thesis

The first paragraph ends with the thesis statement. It states: "By examining the symbols and themes of 'The Cask of Amontillado,' Montresor's inner desire for revenge becomes explicit." The author will highlight instances in which Poe uses symbolism to foreshadow Montresor's act of revenge.

## Argument One

The first symbol the author analyzes is the focus of the first argument. The beginning sentence of this paragraph reads: "The first significant symbol in 'The Cask of Amontillado' is Fortunato's jester costume."

By examining the symbols and themes of "The Cask of Amontillado," Montresor's inner desire for revenge becomes explicit.

The first significant symbol in "The Cask of Amontillado" is Fortunato's jester costume. The imagery of the jester, or fool, is introduced at the carnival as the story begins. Fortunato is described as wearing a "tight-fitting parti-striped dress" and "conical cap and bells."[1] The audience can easily imagine how ridiculous Fortunato looks in this foolish costume, although when he is at the carnival, he does not necessarily stand out. In fact, it is Montresor, described as putting on a mask of black silk and wearing a short, lined cape, who would have looked out of place at the carnival. However, as the story's setting moves to the

Readers are led to imagine Fortunato in a full jester's costume, portraying him as a fool.

catacombs, Fortunato becomes more and more out of place. Fortunato's costume adds an important layer of meaning to the story, as Montresor uses descriptions of the costume to highlight all the ways in which he is superior to Fortunato. The symbolic costume creates irony. Fortunato is not only playing the fool; he is becoming one as well. In addition, Fortunato's costume, which includes bells, sets up the eerie ending of the story when Montresor listens for Fortunato and hears only the jingling of the bells. Fortunato's costume foreshadows how he will become a fool for following Montresor into the catacombs and getting walled up there.

Another symbol used in this short story is the amontillado, which Montresor uses to lure Fortunato into the catacombs. The amontillado and other types of liquor referenced throughout the story symbolize weakness in those who consume it. In fact, in his first description of Fortunato, Montresor

## Argument Two

The author outlines the second symbol for analysis in the next paragraph: "Another symbol used in this short story is the amontillado, which Montresor uses to lure Fortunato into the catacombs." In this argument, the author will highlight the significance of the amontillado.

The cask full of amontillado serves as a symbol for Fortunato's weakness.

notes: "He has a weak point. . . . he prided himself upon his connoisseurship in wine."[2] Fortunato is depicted as having had too much to drink at the carnival party, suggesting his knowledge of wine is not his only weakness; he is known for consuming too much of it as well. As Montresor lures Fortunato away from the party with promises of showing him the amontillado, he continually gives Fortunato wine, keeping him intoxicated. By doing so, Montresor guarantees he will be able to chain up and trap Fortunato without resistance. Liquor represents both a mental and physical weakness in Fortunato, allowing Montresor the upper hand.

Lastly, Montresor's choice to seal Fortunato into the catacombs suggests his revenge is not only for himself but also for the legacy of his family. While Montresor never directly addresses how Fortunato has wronged his family, the recurring symbols of the catacombs and the bones of his family suggest one of Montresor's motivations is revenge on

## Argument Three

The third argument describes the next symbol the author will highlight. The first sentence of this paragraph reads: "Lastly, Montresor's choice to seal Fortunato into the catacombs suggests his revenge is not only for himself but also for the legacy of his family."

behalf of his family. Montresor reveals the significance of trapping Fortunato in the catacombs as they walk through them:

> "The Montresors," I replied, "were a great and numerous family."
>
> "I forget your arms."
>
> "A huge human foot d'or, in a field azure; the foot crushes a serpent rampant whose fangs are imbedded in the heel."
>
> "And the motto?"
>
> "Nemo me impune lacessit."[3]

This Latin motto means, "No one attacks me with impunity." It suggests anyone who injures Montresor's family will not get away with it. The arms, or image that represents a family name, is of a foot crushing a serpent who is biting that same foot. This image reflects how Montresor will seek revenge for his family, much like the foot stomping on the snake, no matter the risk or actual injury. The motto and arms are symbolic of Montresor's thoughts about the act of revenge: he will seek it not only for himself but also for his family's honor, no matter what injuries may result. In fact, Montresor's decision to trap Fortunato in his ancestor's catacombs is symbolic for the same reason: he wants

## Conclusion

In this essay's conclusion, the author sums up the argument by reminding the reader of Poe's use of specific symbols to validate Montresor's act of revenge.

Fortunato to be trapped with his ancestors (represented by the bones in the catacombs) for eternity, as a reminder of the wrongs Fortunato has possibly caused Montresor and his family.

Throughout "The Cask of Amontillado," Poe uses specific symbols to validate Montresor's act of revenge to the reader. After all, in the end, Montresor reveals his revenge against Fortunato has remained undiscovered for half of a century. Montresor feels what might be a moment of guilt when he hears the ringing of the bells as he puts the last stone into the wall, but with that ringing comes the symbolic reminder that Fortunato was a fool who deserved his ultimate fate.

# Thinking Critically

Now it's your turn to assess the essay. Consider these questions:

1.  Do you agree with the argument that Montresor's revenge on Fortunato is deserved? Why, or why not?

2.  Are there any other symbols or imagery in this short story that support or go against the argument in the essay? What are they?

3.  Why does Montresor get away with his revenge? Do you think he deserves to be punished for his actions by Fortunato's family?

# Other Approaches

Reviewing the ways in which symbols are used is just one way to analyze "The Cask of Amontillado." By using other theoretical lenses, there are many other ways to examine the text. One method could include looking at the short story with Poe's biographical history in mind. In addition, one could examine the text in relation to other works of romanticism of the time.

## New Historicist Analysis

Several scholars speculate Poe modeled the character of Fortunato after a contemporary critic who gave him a poor review. By using new historicism, a reader can find a new way to analyze the work. A thesis that reflects this might be: In "The Cask of Amontillado," Poe seeks revenge against the critics who gave his literary work a poor review.

# Romanticism

Another new historicist reading of "The Cask of Amontillado" could focus on romanticism, the literary time period in which Poe wrote. Romantics placed more emphasis on the individual instead of a collective group. A thesis that focuses more specifically on romanticism might read: "The Cask of Amontillado" is written entirely in the perspective of Montresor. By focusing on the internal life of one character, Poe convinces the audience Montresor is justified in his pursuit of revenge.

## 6

## AN OVERVIEW OF
# *True Grit*

*T*he Western genre of literature and film focuses on the wild American frontier. While Westerns tend to be placed historically in the 1800s to the early 1900s, they were particularly popular with audiences through the 1930s to the 1960s. In the early 2000s, their popularity returned with film remakes, such as *3:10 to Yuma* (2007) and *True Grit* (2010). Elements of the Western could also be seen through television shows, such as *Deadwood* (2004–2006). This genre has persisted as uniquely American, and while there are many versions of the Western, they tend to fall into one of several story types. One of these types includes the Western revenge story.

Westerns, which are set on the American frontier, take place in an area of lawlessness. Most often, the

Westerns are infamous for their use of guns and shootouts as a means of revenge and retribution.

Western vengeance story depicts revenge as personal, in which one person seeks revenge on another. The method of revenge is often described as a shootout because of the popularity and vast availability of guns in the West. Westerns also usually focus on maintaining law and order in the wildness of the American west. The main character is typically someone who represents the law—a sheriff or a marshal who overcomes forces of lawlessness and villainy.

## Summary of *True Grit*

*True Grit* is a popular Western novel, written by Charles Portis in 1968. It has been transformed into film twice, once in 1969 starring John Wayne and then in 2010 with Jeff Bridges and Matt Damon. An adult woman named Mattie Ross narrates the book. It begins with Mattie telling a story about when she was 14 years old and found out her father had been shot dead in Fort Smith, Arkansas. The murderer, outlaw Tom Chaney, stole her father's horse, two California gold pieces, and $150.

Mattie's story begins when she goes to Fort Smith to take care of her father's funeral arrangements. While there, she also attempts to find men to pursue Chaney, who she hears has joined a notorious gang led by Lucky

Hailee Steinfeld plays Mattie Ross in the 2010 film.

Ned Piper. Mattie wants Chaney brought back to Fort Smith to be tried for her father's murder. She convinces US Marshal Reuben "Rooster" Cogburn to help her by promising him $100. As soon as Mattie makes these arrangements, Texas Ranger LaBoeuf comes to town hoping to capture Chaney for the murder of a Texas state senator.

## Mattie Joins the Team

LaBoeuf figures out Rooster also intends to find and capture Chaney, so he enlists Rooster's help. Mattie finds this out and also learns of the men's plan to leave her in Fort Smith. Mattie decides to go into Indian Territory to find Chaney on her own, prepping her horse and gathering supplies to leave the next morning. As she sets off, she crosses a river by ferry, where she intercepts Rooster and LaBoeuf. They are appalled to see her and tell the ferryman she is a runaway, resulting in the ferryman kicking her off the ferry. Mattie then finds a place to cross the river on horseback.

Once Mattie is on the other side of the river, Rooster and LaBoeuf capture her, and LaBoeuf begins whipping her. As he does, Rooster threatens LaBoeuf with a gun and forces LaBoeuf to let Mattie go. Mattie appeals to

After Rooster defends Mattie against LaBoeuf, the three travel together to find Tom Chaney.

both of the men, and all three agree to proceed together. They ride throughout the day and come upon a small shelter for the night. However, the shelter is guarded by two thieves, Quincy and Moon, who are waiting with stolen horses for Lucky Ned Piper and the rest of his group to return from a train heist. Rooster and LaBoeuf threaten to arrest them and try persuading the two men to confess the whereabouts of Ned and Chaney.

## Tracking Lucky Ned

Moon begins confessing, which provokes a fight with Quincy, who chops off four of Moon's fingers. Moon then shoots Quincy, and they both die. As soon as Rooster and LaBoeuf clear the bodies, they decide to hide so they can ambush Ned and his gang when they reappear. Rooster hides with Mattie. He tells her many stories of his life, including when he was part of a gang with Frank and Jesse James, the famous bank robbers. Mattie dozes off to sleep but awakens when Ned and the rest of his group arrive. Ned and his group immediately sense something suspicious, and Ned fires warning shots into the air. LaBoeuf shoots at him, giving away his position. In the resulting shootout, four men die, and Ned gets away.

Mattie, LaBoeuf, and Rooster set out to track Ned, thinking Ned will lead them to Chaney. They also plan to stop at a small town nearby, as they have the bodies of those who died in the shootout. They arrive at McAlester's store, and Rooster tries to leave Mattie there, but LaBoeuf argues Mattie has earned the right to stay with them. They transport the bodies to the local police and then head back out. As they ride toward Lucky Ned Piper's hideout, Rooster begins drinking heavily and tells stories to the other two. They stop when Rooster announces they are only four miles (6.4 km) from Ned's hideout.

## Finding Tom Chaney

The next morning, Mattie walks toward a ravine in search of water. She comes across none other than Tom Chaney. Chaney recognizes her right away, and she pulls her gun on him. He grins and mocks her, and Mattie shoots him in the side. She calls out to Rooster and LaBoeuf and tries to shoot Chaney again, but the gun will not fire. Chaney hits Mattie with a piece of wood and starts dragging her toward the hideout. The commotion brings Rooster and LaBoeuf to one side of the ravine, while the other bandits, including Ned, run down the other side. Ned grabs Mattie, warning Rooster and LaBoeuf they have five minutes to leave or he will kill her. Rooster and LaBoeuf agree to leave. Ned takes Mattie to the hideout, where he leaves her with Chaney.

## The Fight

Once Mattie is alone with Chaney, she tries to scald him with hot water. Chaney hits her with his pistol and threatens to throw her into a pit of rattlesnakes. Suddenly, LaBoeuf arrives on the scene, threatening Chaney with a gun. Mattie, Chaney, and LaBoeuf walk out of the hideout, where they see Rooster threatening the other bandits. A shootout begins, and Rooster's horse is shot out from under him. Rooster is suddenly vulnerable, and Ned makes a move to shoot him. LaBoeuf then shoots Ned dead. As this happens, Chaney takes a rock and hits LaBoeuf over the head with it. Mattie then shoots Chaney in the head, but the recoil from the gun sends her down into the pit of snakes.

Mattie becomes stuck in a mossy hole in the pit, with her left arm broken from the fall. She gets her bearings and realizes there is a nest of bats below her. She grabs at a man's shirt she sees in the hole next to her. It turns out the shirt is attached to a man's skeleton, and there is a pile of rattlesnakes inside the skeleton. Mattie, not wanting to slip farther down the hole, breaks off the skeleton's arm and wedges it under her good arm. Then, she uses the skeleton to keep the snakes away from her as they wake up.

Mattie calls out for help, and Chaney appears, alive despite his head wound. As Chaney taunts Mattie, Rooster appears and bashes in Chaney's head. Chaney then falls into the pit toward Mattie, knocking the snakes loose. In the confusion, a rattlesnake bites Mattie. Rooster pulls Mattie out of the pit and races back to Fort Smith to get Mattie to a doctor, leaving LaBoeuf to guard the remaining outlaws.

Rooster shows his loyalty to Mattie when he rescues her from the snake pit.

## The Resolution

Once in Fort Smith, Mattie sees a doctor. She falls in and out of consciousness for the next few days, and the doctor amputates her left arm. Meanwhile, LaBoeuf retrieves Chaney's body from the pit and rides to Texas to deliver the body. As Mattie recovers, she never sees Rooster again, although she hears about his adventures. Many years later, in 1903, Mattie learns Rooster performs in a traveling Wild West show. Hoping to see him, she goes to the show. However, Rooster dies before she gets there. Rooster, having no family, is buried in the town where he died, so Mattie transfers his body to her family's land and reburies him there.

Mattie transfers Rooster's body to be buried by her father's.

# Banding Together for Revenge

*True Grit* is a Western told through the perspective of Mattie Ross, a character seeking revenge against the man who killed her father. The novel's genre is uniquely American. Through *True Grit*, readers can examine ideas and values considered important in US culture in the late 1800s and early 1900s. Because the structure of the Western is so specific, it reveals deeply held American beliefs about how society should be run. One such value is the belief the individual can be more powerful than a group. For example, Westerns often include a rugged individual who seeks justice for those who are weaker and less able. However, in *True Grit*, the American

In *True Grit*, Mattie seeks revenge on the man who murdered her father.

## Thesis

The author's main argument can be found in the last two sentences of the first paragraph: "*True Grit* argues that law, order, and revenge can be maintained only through a group rather than through an individual. Mattie, Rooster, and LaBoeuf must band together in defiance of the typical Western character archetypes to attain their common goal." In this essay, the author will illustrate how the three main characters defy typical Westerns to band together and gain revenge.

## Argument One

The first argument states: "The biggest difference between *True Grit* and other Western vengeance stories is the main character, Mattie." This portion of the essay will elaborate on the characteristics of Mattie that set her apart from the common female and main characters of Westerns.

value of the individual is questioned because there is not one individual but three people—Rooster, LaBoeuf, and Mattie—who must join together to seek retribution against Chaney. *True Grit* argues that law, order, and revenge can be maintained only through a group rather than through an individual. Mattie, Rooster, and LaBoeuf must band together in defiance of the typical Western character archetypes to attain their common goal.

The biggest difference between *True Grit* and other Western vengeance stories is the main character, Mattie. As a 14-year-old girl, Mattie is unlike the traditional main character of Westerns.

Throughout *True Grit*, Mattie gets by with the protection of Rooster and LaBoeuf.

Because the novel is told from the point of view of a girl with very little power in society, she cannot seek justice for her father's death without help from others. Throughout the opening of the story, Mattie's status as a young girl is constantly mentioned. In order to get more respect from the people she encounters, she enlists the help of men—first a lawyer in Arkansas and then Rooster to help her find Chaney. As independent as Mattie is, she is aware her chances of succeeding in finding Chaney are much stronger if she is part of a group rather than going after Chaney alone.

The two men Mattie secures to help her search for Chaney, US Marshal Rooster Cogburn and Texas Ranger LaBoeuf, defy the stereotypical masculine values of Westerns. Each man represents a typical Western male character in his initial actions and appearance. For example, Rooster Cogburn symbolizes a rougher Wild West. After fighting with Confederate

## Argument Two

Argument two states: "The two men Mattie secures to help her search for Chaney, US Marshal Rooster Cogburn and Texas Ranger LaBoeuf, defy the stereotypical masculine values of Westerns." This argument will show how *True Grit*'s two main male characters do not adhere to the traditional structure of the Western.

Rooster often shoots first and asks questions later, painting the picture of the rough Wild Westerner.

soldiers in the American Civil War, Rooster worked to bring outlaws to justice as a US marshal. However, he constantly walks the line between outlaw and lawman himself. He is mostly motivated by money and his own honor. LaBoeuf, who is younger than Rooster, is a Texas ranger who follows laws much more strictly. He has tracked Chaney's movements to Mattie and is interested in capturing him because Chaney murdered a state senator.

But while Rooster and LaBoeuf fit the Western profile in their initial goals, they defy these stereotypes.

First, they travel together, along with Mattie, eliminating the idea of the lone individual. Secondly, they go against the masculine Western stereotype when they allow Mattie, a young and seemingly powerless girl, to join them in their manhunt.

*True Grit* suggests the typical Western individual is limited in keeping order on the frontier, and to keep lasting peace, people—however opposite they are—must work together to achieve revenge. This is demonstrated when Rooster, LaBoeuf, and Mattie must cooperate to capture and kill Chaney. Because Chaney has the protection of Ned's group of bandits, he is more difficult to capture. It takes the collective efforts of Mattie, Rooster, and LaBoeuf to take him down. First, Mattie comes across him in the ravine by Ned's hideout, and because she is a young female, he does not regard her as a threat. But when she is captured, LaBoeuf and Rooster are able to regroup

## Argument Three

The third argument continues the idea that *True Grit* defies the common Western with an individual as the only hero: "*True Grit* suggests the typical Western individual is limited in keeping order on the frontier, and to keep lasting peace, people—however opposite they are—must work together to achieve revenge."

Contrary to most Westerns, in *True Grit*, three main characters must join efforts to seek revenge.

# Conclusion

The arguments conclude in the last two paragraphs of this essay. The conclusion summarizes the ideas that revenge was gained in ways that went against the common Western theme, with a main character of a woman, two men who allow a woman to join them, and their group efforts to attain revenge.

and take Ned and Chaney by surprise, killing them both. In addition, when Mattie is injured and trapped in the pit, it takes both LaBoeuf and Rooster to save her. Rooster then takes Mattie to Fort Smith, while LaBoeuf takes care of Chaney's body. Because Mattie, Rooster, and LaBoeuf work together, all three live, and through the death of Chaney, they are able to reestablish order in their various communities.

Ultimately, the death of Mattie's father is avenged not only through his daughter, Mattie, but also by the two lawmen traveling with her. Although Mattie's quest for revenge did not work out the way she had intended (Cheney never went on trial for the murder of her father), she was able to get justice for his death. The unusual friendship between the three main characters demonstrates a different type of Western, one that places importance on the group to maintain law and order, rather than on the individual.

# Thinking Critically

Now it is your turn to assess the essay. Consider these questions:

1.  Mattie is an unusual main character for a Western. How might this essay change if the story was through the point of view of Rooster, a more traditional Western hero?

2.  This essay addresses Western themes. What other themes of Westerns can be found in *True Grit*?

3.  Are personal vendettas, such as the one Mattie had with Chaney, worthwhile? Does the end justify the means in this case?

# Other Approaches

Contemporary scholars have worked to analyze Westerns, particularly because of their popularity. Arguments that have been made about other Westerns could also be applied to *True Grit*. Some other issues to explore include how Mattie's desire for revenge shapes her role in society as a woman and how Rooster's status as both an outlaw seeking revenge and a lawman allows him to be accepting of Mattie and her goal.

## Feminist Criticism

*True Grit* is told from the point of view of Mattie years after the events have taken place. Mattie is now an unmarried and successful businesswoman. A thesis that considers Mattie's unusual role as a woman in the Wild West might read: Mattie's desire for revenge for her father's death is a formative event that influences her decisions later in life, allowing her to become a successful, independent woman.

## Character Analysis

In this novel, characters often defy the archetypal Western roles. Rooster seems to fit the archetype of the outlaw who wanders from place to place in search of revenge, even if he attempts to be representative of the lawman. A thesis that focuses on Rooster's role in the novel might be: In *True Grit*, Rooster can be considered both a lawman and an outlaw seeking revenge. It is this outsider status that allows him to be accepting of Mattie, another character who defies stereotypes and also pursues revenge.

## 8

AN OVERVIEW OF

# *The Princess Bride*

*T*he *Princess Bride* is a 1987 film adaptation of William Goldman's 1973 book *The Princess Bride: S. Morgenstern's Classic Tale of True Love and High Adventure.* The film begins with a grandfather reading the book to his sick grandson. The tale begins with Westley, a farm boy, and a maid, Buttercup, falling in love. Westley decides to go to sea in order to find fortune, though he plans to one day return to the farm and marry Buttercup. However, on his journey, pirates attack Westley's ship, and he is presumed killed by the Dread Pirate Roberts.

Robin Wright plays Buttercup in the 1987 film
*The Princess Bride.*

## Buttercup's Kidnapping

Five years later, Buttercup is engaged to marry Prince Humperdinck, though she does not love him. On one of her daily horseback rides, three men, Vizzini, the ringleader, Fezzik, the giant, and Inigo Montoya, the Spaniard, kidnap Buttercup. As the men sail away with Buttercup, a masked man attempts to stop them. Inigo Montoya corners the masked man and duels with him. Montoya loses, but the masked man spares his life. Montoya explains his sole purpose in life is to become a skilled swordsman so he can find the six-fingered man who killed his father and take revenge on him. The masked man next evades Fezzik and tricks Vizzini into drinking poison, killing him. The masked man then saves Buttercup, and she discovers he is her lost love, Westley.

## Westley's Capture

As soon as they are reunited, Westley and Buttercup must flee Prince Humperdinck, who is tracking them. They enter the Fire Swamp, where Westley becomes injured, and Buttercup convinces him to surrender to Prince Humperdinck. The prince promises he will return Westley to his ship, but instead he has Westley chained

Westley comes back and saves Buttercup from her kidnappers.

up by Count Tyrone Rugen and attached to a machine that tortures him, taking away years of his life.

Meanwhile, Montoya and Fezzik realize the six-fingered man who killed Montoya's father is Count Rugen, the man torturing Westley. Arriving at the castle, they find Westley dead and the count nowhere to be seen. The men take Westley to Miracle Max in hope of bringing Westley back to life. When Miracle Max learns Westley must come back to life to win back Buttercup, he revives Westley. He also hates Prince Humperdinck. Together, Westley, Montoya, and Fezzik plan to stop Humperdinck's marriage to Buttercup.

In true fairy tale fashion, Westley protects Buttercup in the Fire Swamp.

## Happily Ever After

As Westley slowly regains the use of his faculties, he, Montoya, and Fezzik devise a plan to storm the castle and stop the wedding. While Westley and Fezzik look for Buttercup, Montoya finds Count Rugen, the six-fingered man, and challenges him to a swordfight in order to seek revenge. Montoya, while gravely wounded from the fight, avenges his father's death by killing Count Rugen. Buttercup, thinking Westley is dead, finds a dagger to kill herself. Westley stops her just in time, and they reunite. Prince Humperdinck finds the two of them, and even though Westley has not recovered control of his body, he convinces Prince Humperdinck to flee the room, telling him that if they were to duel, Westley would leave him alive but maimed. At the end of the tale, Westley, Buttercup, Fezzik, and Montoya all flee the castle on horses, and Westley and Buttercup live happily ever after.

# 9

# Anti-Revenge in *The Princess Bride*

The movie *The Princess Bride* features a grandfather telling his grandson the romance story of Buttercup and Westley. By bookending the film with the grandfather and grandson reading the story together, the filmmakers demonstrate that this story is meant to be shared between people—as the grandfather shares it with his grandson—in order to educate and entertain others. Analyzing the film in this light is an example of narrative criticism, a method of analysis that focuses on the way in which the plot of a story affects and instructs the audience.

While Inigo, *right*, is driven by revenge, Westley, *left*, is driven by his love for Buttercup.

Narrative criticism focuses on the features of the story that further its message. These features might include setting, characters, narrator (if there is one), major events, and genre. Once the message of the story is determined, the author can construct an argument about whether the story is effective. In narrative criticism, it is important to consider the discourse of the story—the way the narrative is presented to the audience through its point of view, style, and overall effect. In addition, the genre of the story can be a beginning point for analysis.

In *The Princess Bride*, each character is guided by his or her own goals: Westley and Buttercup are compelled by true love; Prince Humperdinck and Vizzini are motivated by greed; and Inigo Montoya is driven by revenge. Montoya's drive to get revenge on his father's killer is a particularly important subplot. By comparing Montoya's motivation of revenge and Vizzini and Prince

## *Thesis*

The thesis of this essay states: "By comparing Montoya's motivation of revenge and Vizzini and Prince Humperdinck's motivation of greed to Westley and Buttercup's motivation of true love, the story portrays revenge as an empty and meaningless pursuit." This essay will focus on the ways *The Princess Bride* can be interpreted with an anti-revenge theme.

Humperdinck's motivation of greed to Westley and Buttercup's motivation of true love, the story portrays revenge as an empty and meaningless pursuit.

Westley and Buttercup, the main characters of the story, are ultimately motivated by true love, and because of this, they prosper at the end of the film. Westley begins as a poor boy who falls in love with Buttercup. When he is kidnapped by pirates and cannot return home to her, he becomes the hero of the story, and his actions drive the story along. His main motivation—love—is opposed to greed and revenge, the motivations of the other characters. Because of this, Westley succeeds where others fail. In fact, true love saves his life on several occasions, particularly when Montoya and Fezzik rescue him from the torture machine. When they take Westley to Miracle Max in the hope he can bring Westley back to life, Max is compelled to do so because his wife overhears Westley's

## Argument One

The first argument states: "Westley and Buttercup, the main characters of the story, are ultimately motivated by true love, and because of this, they prosper at the end of the film." This argument will highlight Westley and Buttercup's success as a result of their drive for true love.

After being saved from the torture machine, Westley is brought back to life because of his love for Buttercup.

reason for returning to life is true love and because he himself seeks revenge on Prince Humperdinck.

Buttercup also becomes a better person because of her desire for true love. In the opening scenes of the film, she constantly orders Westley around. However, when she realizes she is in love with him, she becomes a kinder person, as demonstrated by a scene in which she adds "please" to a command she gives him. When Westley is presumed dead, Buttercup is devastated and accepts a proposal of marriage from Prince Humperdinck. However, when she and Westley are captured, Buttercup agrees to marry Humperdinck on the condition that he keep Westley alive—sparing her own desire for true love in exchange for Westley's life. She immediately regrets this decision, as evidenced by a dream. In this dream, Buttercup is being presented to the kingdom, and everyone bows down to her except for one old woman, who boos her. The old woman chides Buttercup for having love and giving it up. She reminds Buttercup that true love saved her in the Fire Swamp and that if she marries another man while her true love lives, she is nothing but garbage. When Buttercup wakes, she tells Humperdinck she cannot marry him. Ultimately, it is her love of Westley that allows her to escape Humperdinck.

Vizzini and Prince Humperdinck, who are both motivated by greed for power, do not achieve their goals, as Vizzini is killed and Humperdinck is forced to flee. Vizzini, a villain who kidnaps Buttercup on behalf of Prince Humperdinck,

## Argument Two

The next argument introduces the secondary characters considered for analysis: "Vizzini and Prince Humperdinck, who are both motivated by greed for power, do not achieve their goals, as Vizzini is killed and Humperdinck is forced to flee."

does so for the money such a task gives him. He is ordered to kill Buttercup and frame a neighboring kingdom so that a war is justified between the two kingdoms. His scheme is interrupted by the masked man in black (Westley), who physically overcomes both Fezzik and Montoya. Vizzini is outwitted by Westley and tricked into drinking poison. His power and pride allowed him to think he was smarter and, therefore, more powerful than Westley, proving fatal.

Prince Humperdinck has a similar greed for power. He plans to marry Buttercup and then have her murdered to get his people to go to war. In going to war, Humperdinck will become a more powerful ruler. However, Westley ruins his plan. Weak from being killed and then brought back to life, Westley verbally threatens Humperdinck until he surrenders.

Inigo Montoya is motivated by revenge, but his character does not develop, revealing that his quest for revenge is shallow. Montoya's main motivation for his actions is finding the six-fingered man who

## Argument Three

The last argument of the essay focuses on Inigo Montoya and his motivations in the story: "Inigo Montoya is motivated by revenge, but his character does not develop, revealing that his quest for revenge is shallow."

*Vizzini, left, is outwitted and killed after kidnapping Buttercup.*

killed his father and seeking revenge on him. At the end of the film, Montoya admits as much, saying, "You know, it's very strange, I've been in the revenge business for so long, now that it's over, I don't know what to do with the rest of my life."[1] Montoya always follows others because he is so driven by his singular goal that he cannot act for himself. In fact, his desire for revenge is so well known that it becomes a running joke throughout the film. He continually repeats, "Hello. My name is Inigo Montoya. You killed my father; prepare to die."[2] When he gains his goal, he is left with nothing. Montoya's example is not one to follow, and through this story, the audience is taught revenge is an empty goal.

By the end of *The Princess Bride*, the boy being told the story in the film, who also stands in for the audience, understands revenge is not a worthwhile pursuit because even if that goal is achieved, it does not allow for growth of character. Through analyzing the goals and narrative arcs of the characters in *The Princess Bride*, Inigo Montoya stands out as a character who is unable to change because of his one goal of revenge. Since the film is able to communicate this message through the actions of the characters, it is successful in sharing this message with the boy and, therefore, the audience: revenge is a meaningless and empty goal.

## Conclusion

Finally, the essay concludes, summarizing the author's thesis and main arguments about the theme of revenge in *The Princess Bride*.

# Thinking Critically

Now it is your turn to assess the essay. Consider these questions:

1. The essay argues the characters who have the motive of true love end up being redeemed. Do you agree with this argument? Can you think of any characters for which this does not end up being true?

2. *The Princess Bride* exhibits many archetypes often found in love stories, such as Buttercup as the damsel in distress. What other character archetypes can you find in *The Princess Bride*?

3. What effect does the story within the story in the film have on the viewer's experience of watching it? Does it help the story? If so, how? If not, why does it take away from the story?

# Other Approaches

Film can offer a variety of opportunities for critical analysis. Some areas of consideration in analyzing *The Princess Bride* include looking at how the women are portrayed throughout the film and how the film incorporates the characteristics of the romance genre. It is also worth considering how these two topics affect the role of revenge.

## Archetypal Analysis

In *The Princess Bride*, there are many characters who adhere to hero and villain stereotypes. For example, while Westley is the traditional hero, Vizzini and Humperdinck are the villains. However, not all characters fit into these typical roles. A thesis that considers Montoya and his desire for revenge might be: Inigo Montoya's desire for revenge in *The Princess Bride* makes him morally ambivalent. Therefore, when he is working with Vizzini, a villain, he also becomes a villain.

## The Romance Genre

*The Princess Bride* is considered a romance, although it is not entirely such. Part of narrative criticism involves considering how genre shapes the way an audience receives the story. Knowing *The Princess Bride* is a romance helps interpret how the characters act and how the plot will play out in the story. The audience expects supernatural and epic events to take place, as well as for good to triumph over evil. A possible thesis based on the genre of *The Princess Bride* might be: Because *The Princess Bride* is a romance, the themes surrounding love in the film highly contrast the theme of revenge.

# Analyze It!

Now that you have examined the theme of revenge, are you ready to perform your own analysis? You have read that this type of evaluation can help you look at literature in a new way and make you pay attention to certain issues you may not have otherwise recognized. So, why not look for a revenge theme in one or more of your favorite books?

First, choose the work you want to analyze. Who is the main character? Are there secondary characters? Do characters grow or change through quests for revenge? If you choose to compare the theme in more than one work, what do they have in common? How do they differ? Next, write a specific question about the theme that interests you. Then you can form your thesis, which should provide the answer to that question. Your thesis is the most important part of your analysis and offers an argument about the work, considering the theme, its effect on the characters, or what it says about society or the world. Recall that the thesis statement typically appears at the very end of the introductory paragraph of your essay. It is usually only one sentence long.

After you have written your thesis, find evidence to back it up. Good places to start are in the work itself or in journals or articles that discuss what other people have said about it. You may also want to read about the author or creator's life so you can get a sense of what factors may have affected the creative process. This can be especially useful if you are considering how the theme connects to history or the author's intent.

You should also explore parts of the book that seem to disprove your thesis and create an argument against them. As you do this, you might want to address what others have written about the book. Their quotes may help support your claim.

Before you start analyzing a work, think about the different arguments made in this book. Reflect on how evidence supporting the thesis was presented. Did you find that some of the techniques used to back up the arguments were more convincing than others? Try these methods as you prove your thesis in your own critique.

When you are finished writing your critique, read it over carefully. Is your thesis statement understandable? Do the supporting arguments flow logically, with the topic of each paragraph clearly stated? Can you add any information that would present your readers with a stronger argument in favor of your thesis? Were you able to use quotes from the book, as well as from other critics, to enhance your ideas? Did you see the work in a new light?

# Glossary

### antagonist
A person who opposes another person.

### benefactor
Someone who helps someone else by giving money.

### catacomb
An underground place where bodies are buried.

### chide
To gently scold.

### crypt
A room under a church in which bodies are buried.

### exploit
To use someone or something in a way that unfairly helps you.

### genre
A particular category of literature or film.

### grisly
Involving shock and horror.

### impunity
Free from harm.

### macabre
Involving death or fear.

### monologue
A long speech made by one person.

### reaffirm
To assert strongly again.

### recoil
The pushback from a gun.

### soliloquy
A speech in which a character talks to oneself or is unaware of the presence of others.

# Characteristics
## AND CLASSICS

Revenge is a common theme in literature. The theme of revenge is often depicted through a character who finds him- or herself in a circumstance that makes him or her aware of a need for revenge. In some works, revenge is depicted as successful retribution, and in others, such as tragedies, revenge can end in a character's downfall.

## This theme often includes:

- A main character who seeks revenge
- A character who serves as the main character's rival
- A bittersweet or tragic ending
- Challenges or obstacles the main character must overcome

## Some famous works with a revenge theme are:

- Homer's *The Iliad*
- Alexandre Dumas's *The Count of Monte Cristo*
- Charles Dickens's *Great Expectations*
- F. Scott Fitzgerald's *The Great Gatsby*
- John Grisham's *A Time to Kill*
- Suzanne Collins's *Mockingjay*
- Gillian Flynn's *Gone Girl*

# References

Baym, Nina, ed. *The Norton Anthology of American Literature 1820–1865.* 6th ed. New York: Norton, 2002. Print.

Poe, Edgar Allen. "The Cask of Amontillado." *The Norton Anthology of American Literature, 1820–1865.* 6th ed. Nina Baym, ed. New York: Norton, 2002. Print.

Portis, Charles. *True Grit.* New York: Overlook, 1968. Print.

*The Princess Bride,* Dir. Rob Reiner. 20th Century Fox, 1987. Film.

Shakespeare, William. "Hamlet." *Shakespeare: Four Great Tragedies.* Sylvan Barnet, ed. New York: Signet, 1982. Print.

Shakespeare, William. "Othello." *Shakespeare: Four Great Tragedies.* Alvin Kernen, ed. New York: Signet, 1982. Print.

# Additional
## RESOURCES

### Further Readings

Bloom, Harold, ed. *William Shakespeare, Tragedies*. New York: Infobase Learning, 2009. Print.

Cogburn, Brett. *Rooster: The Life and Time of the Real Rooster Cogburn, the Man Who Inspired True Grit*. New York: Kensington, 2012. Print.

Corrigan, Timothy. *Short Guide to Writing about Film*. 9th ed. New York: Pearson, 2014. Print.

Elwes, Cary. *As You Wish: Inconceivable Tales from the Making of The Princess Bride*. New York: Touchstone, 2014. Print.

Johnson, Claudia. *Social and Psychological Disorder in the Works of Edgar Allen Poe*. Farmington Hills, MI: Gale, 2010. Print.

### Websites

To learn more about Essential Literary Themes, visit **booklinks.abdopublishing.com**. These links are routinely monitored and updated to provide the most current information available.

## Places to Visit

**The Academy of Motion Picture Arts
and Sciences Museum**
8949 Wilshire Boulevard
Beverly Hills, CA 90211
310-247-3000
http://www.oscars.org
The museum embraces the interdisciplinary approach of
filmmaking and how it combines theater, literature, photography,
painting, music, and other art forms.

**Folger Shakespeare Library**
201 East Capitol Street, SE
Washington, DC 20003
202-544-4600
http://www.folger.edu
Watch performances and learn more about the life and works of
William Shakespeare.

**The Poe Museum**
1914-16 East Main Street
Richmond, VA 23223
804-648-5523
http://www.poemuseum.org
Located just blocks away from Edgar Allen Poe's first home in
Richmond, the Poe Museum is filled with Poe's manuscripts and
letters as well as other personal belongings.

# Source Notes

## Chapter 1. Introduction to Themes in Literature

1. Francis Bacon. "On Revenge." *The Essays of Francis Bacon.* Mary Augusta Scott, ed. New York: Scribner, 1908. Print.

## Chapter 2. An Overview of *Hamlet* and *Othello*

1. William Shakespeare. "Hamlet." *Shakespeare: Four Great Tragedies.* Sylvan Barnet, ed. New York: Signet, 1982. Print. 634.

## Chapter 3. Vengeful Characters

1. William Shakespeare. "Othello." *Shakespeare: Four Great Tragedies*. Alvin Kernen, ed. New York: Signet, 1982. Print. 321.

2. William Shakespeare. "Hamlet." *Shakespeare: Four Great Tragedies*. Sylvan Barnet, ed. New York: Signet, 1982. Print. 91–93.

3. William Shakespeare. "Othello." *Shakespeare: Four Great Tragedies*. Alvin Kernen, ed. New York: Signet, 1982. Print.171–174.

4. William Shakespeare. "Hamlet." *Shakespeare: Four Great Tragedies*. Sylvan Barnet, ed. New York: Signet, 1982. Print. 444.

5. William Shakespeare. "Othello." *Shakespeare: Four Great Tragedies*. Alvin Kernen, ed. New York: Signet, 1982. Print. 432.

6. Ibid. 424.

7. Eleanor Prosser. *Hamlet and Revenge*. 2nd ed. Stanford: Stanford UP, 1971. Print. 4–5.

## Chapter 4. An Overview of "The Cask of Amontillado"

1. Edgar Allen Poe. "The Cask of Amontillado." *The Norton Anthology of American Literature*, 1820–1865. 6th ed. Nina Baym, ed. New York: Norton, 2002. Print. 1567

2. Ibid.

## Chapter 5. Symbolic Revenge

1. Edgar Allen Poe. "The Cask of Amontillado." *The Norton Anthology of American Literature*, 1820–1865. 6th ed. Nina Baym, ed. New York: Norton, 2002. Print. 1593.
2. Ibid.
3. Ibid. 1595.

## Chapter 6. An Overview of *True Grit*

None.

## Chapter 7. Banding Together for Revenge

None.

## Chapter 8. An Overview of *The Princess Bride*

None.

## Chapter 9. Anti-Revenge in *The Princess Bride*

1. *The Princess Bride*, Dir. Rob Reiner. 20th Century Fox, 1987. Film.
2. Ibid.

# Index

# About the Author

Caitlin Ray lives in Omaha, Nebraska, where she is pursuing a master's degree in English at the University of Nebraska at Omaha. Her area of focus is composition and rhetoric, with a specialty in disability studies. She teaches in the first-year writing program at the university and has worked as a reading teacher for the Institute of Reading Development. In addition, she has worked as an actor and as an actor-educator at CLIMB Theatre.